THE GHOSTLY TALES OF ORLANDO

This book is dedicated to:
My wife Jen and Tinker Bell the Shih Tzu, both of whom often join me on my strange travels;
my nephews, Adam and Seth, who I kept in mind while writing these ghostly tales; and
all curious readers, however young or old, who make sharing spooky stories so much fun.

Published by Arcadia Children's Books
A Division of Arcadia Publishing, Inc.
Charleston, SC
www.arcadiapublishing.com

Spooky America is a trademark of Arcadia Publishing, Inc.
First published in 2025

Manufactured in the United States

Designed by Jessica Nevins
Images used courtesy of Shutterstock.com; p. 66 JennLShoots/Shutterstock.com.

ISBN: 9781467196024
Library of Congress Control Number: 2025936377

Spooky America

THE GHOSTLY TALES OF ORLANDO

JOSHUA GINSBERG

Adapted from *Haunted Orlando* by Joshua Ginsberg

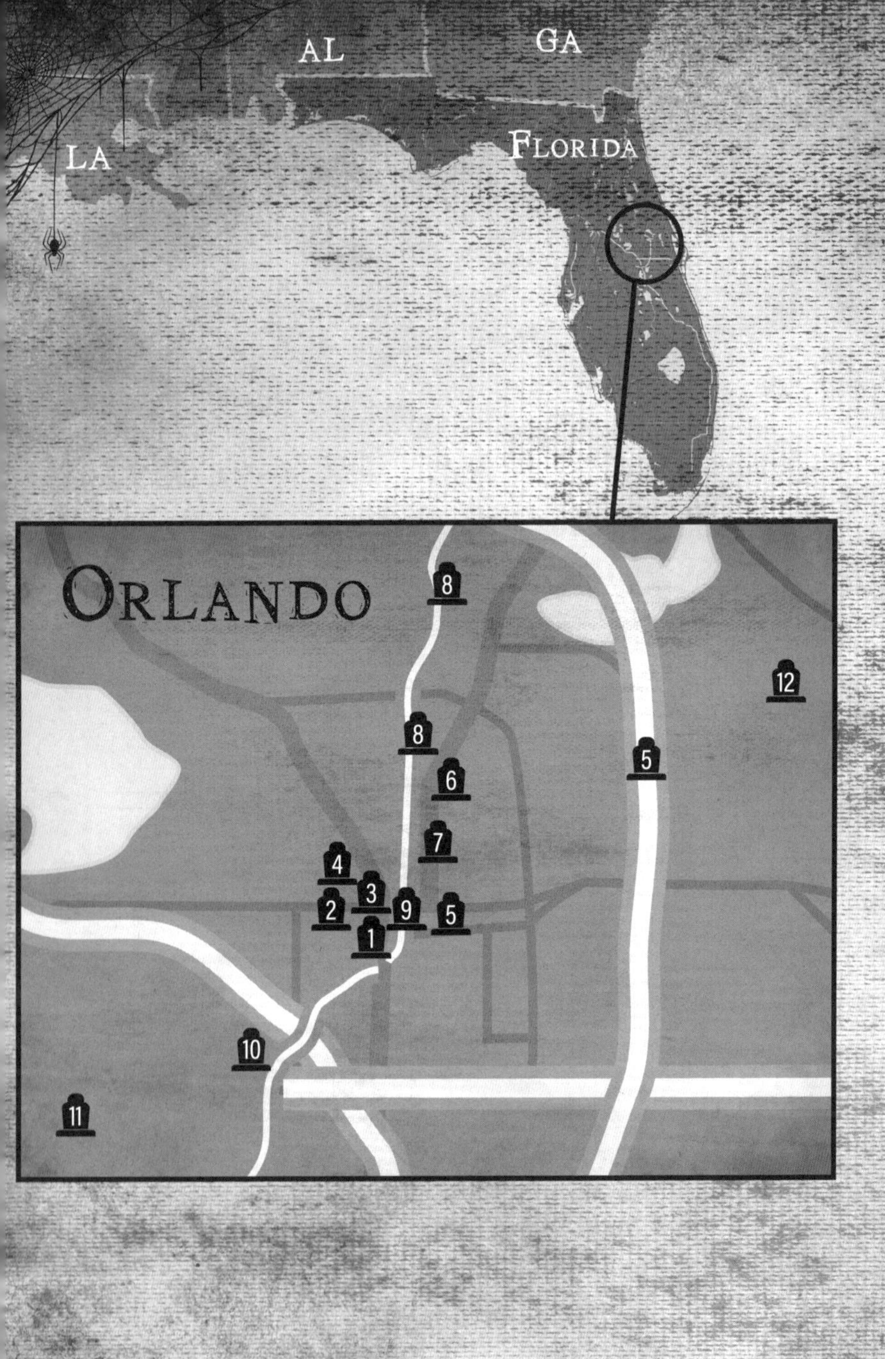
AL
GA
LA
FLORIDA
ORLANDO
8
8
12
5
6
7
4
3
2
9
5
1
10
11

Table of Contents & Map Key

Welcome to Spooky Orlando!

If you and I were going to spend the day together, absolutely anywhere, where would you want to go? Would you choose a place that has parks, beaches, and other outdoor activities? Would a big city with shopping and restaurants most excite you, or a small town with lots of history? Museums and libraries, perhaps? What about some of the biggest and most exciting theme parks on the planet, with rollercoasters and fantastic rides; a place where you could have fun with your favorite characters from movies and comic books? Would you believe me if I told you there's a city in Central Florida that has all these things—and MORE? Well, there is!

Welcome to Orlando, Florida, or—as locals sometimes call it: "The City Beautiful" or "O-Town." They love the great food, art, and culture the city has to offer. But there's another reason Orlando is famous; one that brings more than *seventy million* people here every single year. Home to world-renowned Disney theme parks like Magic Kingdom, Epcot, Hollywood Studios, and Animal Kingdom, not to mention Universal Studios, Legoland, Old Town, Volcano Bay, and many other attractions, it's no *wonder* Orlando is known as the Theme Park Capital of the World. In Orlando, you can visit Cinderella's castle, sparkling against the Florida sky. You can fly on a broomstick alongside your friends at the Wizarding World of Harry Potter, or take a ride on the Orlando Eye at ICON Park, the city's iconic four-hundred-foot-high Ferris wheel. From underwater kingdoms to futuristic cities to lands made entirely of colorful building blocks, each park is its own world.

(That sounds like fun, doesn't it?!)

But what if I told you that many of those same attractions—including restaurants, hotels, museums, and other locations—are

haunted? Would that change your mind about wanting to visit Orlando? I hope not. In fact, if you're anything like me . . . it might make you want to see it even *more*.

So, let's look for those ghosts and spirits together. Some of them, such as the ghost of a young girl named Emily, are playful and happy to interact with us. Others, like the ghosts of Annie Russell and Gordon Rogers, are keeping an eye on the places they loved when they were alive. A few of them aren't nice at all. (But don't worry about those ghosts, because you and I will keep each other safe.) If we *do* get scared, we can always turn on another light to keep the ghosts away. Just remember, like us, each of the spirits we will encounter has their own story and their own reasons for continuing to linger among the living.

There's no need to be alarmed if you see something unexpected, like a shadow that seems to move on its own, or a face pressed up to the glass of a window, watching you from an otherwise-dark room. (And if you come back to your hotel and find the outline of someone already lying in your bed, just give them some space.)

As long as you treat these special guests with the same respect that you would show a living fellow traveler, they won't cause you any trouble or follow you home. So grab your flashlight and fasten your seatbelt—it's time to meet some ghosts!

The Ghost of Gertrude Sweet

Has your local newspaper ever recognized you for your creativity, athletic ability, a school project, or some other skill or quality? If so, you can understand how someone might want to hold on to that moment and make sure other people remember it, too. The thing is, some people hold on a little too long after their moment has passed—even after *they've* passed on!

Is that what's happening with Gertrude Sweet? After all, a local newspaper once called her "the most beautiful woman in Orange County." It seems like she still wants everyone to know it.

Gertrude was born in 1862. She moved to Orlando when she was thirteen years old, joining her older siblings, including her brother Charles, who would be elected Mayor of Orlando in 1881. Before he became mayor, though, one of his first major jobs was to plan

many of the city's roads and streets. He named the widest one, "Gertrude's Avenue," after his sister.

In 1883, Gertrude married a musician named Henry Newell. Together, they raised three children. Her life appears to have been a happy one, although she was disappointed when railroad tracks were laid through the beautiful, wide street with her name on it.

In 1980, thirty-five years after Gertrude was laid to rest, the city decided to honor her with a new path known as "Gertrude's Walk," connecting to Orlando's Urban Trail. Signs along the walk include an image of Gertrude wearing Victorian period clothing, including a parasol over her shoulder. Even if the images don't capture her brown hair and bright blue eyes, it's easy to tell that she was a stylish woman in her day.

If she was a proud woman in life, it seems she may be even *more* so in her afterlife. A local ghost tour guide says Gertrude once went along with a bridal party to see some of the city's haunted hot spots. The bride apparently said something unflattering about Gertrude's appearance based on her image on the sign, and for the rest of the night, the bride had an awful time. She felt invisible hands scratching her, pushing her, and pulling at her dress and hair. Other young women have recalled similar experiences. Some have felt the air around them suddenly become very chilly, or had the distinct and unpleasant feeling of being watched. Others claim to have been pushed and pulled by unseen forces.

If you're near Gertrude's Walk and happen to catch a scent of rose perfume, it's possible her ghost might be somewhere nearby. When Gertrude is around, you must not say anything insulting or unkind about her. If you stick to that one simple rule, she will probably just continue on her way and allow you to go on yours.

A Night at the Museum with Emily

Can you picture what Orlando might have looked like fifty, or a hundred, or even a thousand years ago? Before all the roller coasters, water slides, and castles? Try to imagine this place without any tall buildings, busy highways, or amusement parks. Pretty hard to imagine, isn't it?

That's where the Orange County Regional History Center comes to the rescue!

This family-friendly museum takes you on a time-traveling adventure into Orlando's past. Through fascinating exhibits full of real artifacts, you'll discover what Orlando was like long ago, before anyone ever built the first railroad tracks, planted the first orange trees, or drew the first pictures of cartoon mice named Mickey and Minnie.

The center is housed in a historic building with impressive columns. Built in 1927, it was originally part of a courthouse where judges decided actual cases. The original courthouse—where many famous trials took place—was demolished years ago, but the can't-miss columns still stand today.

Since the museum opened in 2000, it has brought Orlando's past back to life—some say perhaps a little *too* well! During the day, you can wander the halls and rooms, including a recreation of one of the courtrooms from the original building. If reports are true, though, overnight visitors get a different experience. Imagine walking through a hallway when suddenly—*BRRR!*—you hit an icy-cold pocket of air that makes you shiver! Or watching the elevators rise and fall, doors opening with a *ding*, even when nobody has pressed any buttons. You might hear—but not see—someone pacing the floor of that model courtroom.

Other odd things have happened here, too. Some visitors feel tiny goosebumps pop up on their arms or the hair on the back of their necks suddenly stand up, as if somebody is watching them from behind. Others hear the giggling of a young girl coming from just around a corner, but when they rush to look—nobody is there! Objects vanish or move from their places, only to show up somewhere completely different later. And if you are exceedingly lucky (or maybe unlucky, depending how you feel about ghosts), you might even catch a glimpse of Emily—the ghost girl known to wander the museum's halls after everyone has gone home.

Nobody knows for sure how Emily died or why she has taken up residence in the museum. Some speculate that she is attached to the replica courthouse because the original room might have been the last place she saw her family before becoming a ward of the state. The sad story goes that she caught pneumonia—a serious illness that makes it hard to breathe—and died before she could reunite with them.

These days, when visitors spot Emily, she appears as a little girl in a simple white dress with her dark hair in pigtails. Some believe that she is only eleven or twelve years old, but Ting Rappa, who leads American Ghost Adventures, believes that she is closer to seven or eight. Rappa should know! After all, she and her team have been communicating with Emily ever since they began investigating the building's strange happenings back in 2004. Since then, they have developed a special relationship with the shy ghost. Emily can't talk like we do, but she has figured out other ways to communicate. Sometimes she'll flick the team's flashlights on and off—once for "yes" and twice for "no"—to answer questions. Other times, Ting and the other investigators

discover messages Emily has left them on their voice recorders.

Following their initial interaction with Emily, Rappa and her ghost-hunting team began leaving objects for their invisible friend. They'd place candy and frosted animal crackers around the museum after all the guests had gone home. These sweet surprises seemed to make Emily happy—whenever they left special items, she would become more interactive. Lights would flicker more frequently, and their equipment would pick up hints of ghostly whispers or even laughter.

One summer, after the museum hosted a camp slumber party, Rappa and her team discovered that Emily had been watching the children at play and very much seemed to want a toy of her own. The American Ghost

Adventures team left a small teddy bear for Emily that she still seems very fond of to this day. When it is placed somewhere for her to play with, she is more likely to respond to and interact with the living.

In fact, Emily became so fond of her toy that it briefly became a source of trouble for one of Rappa's tour guides. One frigid night in December, when the guide was closing up, she accidentally put Emily's stuffed animal in one of her personal bags and left the building with it.

From the moment this young woman left the building, she began experiencing unexplained problems with her electronic devices and appliances, including her phone, her hair dryer, her television, and even her car! Eventually, she located Emily's prized possession and returned it to the museum. Emily must have been satisfied with her toy's return, because from that moment on, all the tour guide's electronics went back to working properly.

Sometime later, Rappa's team received confirmation that Emily was behind the electronics malfunctions. They brought a medium to the museum—a person with a special ability to talk with spirits, and who the spirits sometimes speak *through*, too. During the visit, something incredible happened. The medium's voice suddenly changed, becoming higher and more childlike. Emily was speaking through the medium directly to Rappa and her team!

First, she asked the tour guide who used to leave animal crackers for her: "Why don't you bring me the treats I like anymore?" Then, the medium turned to the tour guide who had accidentally taken the teddy bear. "I bet you won't do that again," Emily said, still speaking through the medium. "I needed to teach you a lesson. It's my toy!"

Ever since, you can be certain every tour guide has double-checked their bags before leaving the museum to make sure they haven't accidentally taken Emily's precious stuffed animal.

Another spooky detail: Emily doesn't always stay put in the museum. Sometimes, she gets curious and follows visitors all the way to their cars in the parking lot! In fact, that very thing happened once to Rappa herself. One night, as she left the museum and got into her van, her infant son's toys suddenly began flashing their lights and making sounds. Rappa froze—she hadn't touched any of them! Realizing it had to be Emily, Rappa politely asked her to return to the museum, promising to visit again soon. As soon as she did so, all the toys went silent and dark.

Emily usually prefers to stay within her museum home's walls. She's also not the only ghost roaming these historic halls—it seems Emily has some "spirited" roommates! One is believed to be the ghost of a restless juror who died before he could share his verdict on an important case. If you listen closely, some people say you can hear the *tap-tap-tapping* of his invisible footsteps as he paces back and forth across the floor of the old courtroom.

Another friendly spirit may be a former bailiff, Arnold Wilkerson, who died tragically in the building when a deranged and violent man shot and killed him in 1984. (A bailiff is an officer of the court, who makes sure everyone follows the rules and stays safe while the judge is working.) Since then, several visitors have experienced a feeling of being watched over in a protective way, and at least one person has heard a voice ask them if they needed any help. If you hear the same voice, don't be alarmed. That's just Arnie, still faithfully watching over his courthouse, even decades after his death.

The Ghost of George Rogers

If you ask a real estate agent what makes a property worth lots of money, they'll probably grin and say, "Location, location, and location!" Well, guess what? The same rule applies to haunted buildings! And when it comes to eerie locations within and around the city of Orlando, you won't find a better spot for a haunting than the corner of East Pine Street and South Magnolia Avenue. In fact, there has been so much supernatural activity here that some people believe it is cursed!

Stand on this corner for just five minutes, and you'll understand why it gives people the shivers. Without warning, you may feel an unexpected gust of icy air—even on the hottest Florida afternoon—or hear strange whispers or muffled cries when no one is around. You might spot shadows stretching into unfamiliar shapes, or feel like someone, or *something*, is watching you from a nearby building window overlooking the same corner. Believe it or not, on the corner of East Pine and South Magnolia, you would not be the first to experience such things!

But why is that corner thought to be cursed? The answer might lie buried in Orlando's past. Some older sources suggest this was the site of Orlando's first graveyard, where the Union Free Church once stood. There could have been an even older Indigenous burial mound there. Another reason might be that the most devastating fire in Orlando's history started nearby, inside a grocery store on Pine and Main Street in 1884. Finally, some believe that the intersection is where two streams of mystical energy called "ley lines" cross. (Think of them as supernatural highways that spirits might travel along!)

Whatever makes this corner so ghostly, one thing's for certain: every building standing here has experienced some strange or unexplainable paranormal event. The most famous of these spooky spots also happens to be the oldest building in the city, the historic Rogers Building.

An English settler named Gordon Rogers designed the building, which housed his store and also served as a place for his British friends to hang out. These men so often gathered that they formed a group called the English Club, with the Rogers building as their official meeting place. Like many clubs of that time period, membership was restricted to men only. This meant that George's wife was not allowed to join their meetings or activities. But now, all these years later, some believe it is her turn to have full access to the place that once excluded her—as the building's most famous ghost!

It's hard to say when people began to notice strange happenings at the Rogers Building. Decades after George and his wife had passed away, the building became a dance studio, where some of the dancers experienced odd

things. When practicing or dancing along, they would suddenly feel invisible fingers touching their shoulders, or phantom hands gently guiding their arms—as if a ghost had decided to join their dance! When the building was turned into a small movie theater, people regularly complained about their personal items disappearing, only to have them later turn up somewhere else in the building.

Perhaps the creepiest experience happened during the building's time as the Mad Cow Theater. One night, right in the middle of a play, an actress spotted a police officer escorting an elderly woman across the middle of the stage. The actress was completely confused—why would anyone interrupt the play like that? Imagine her surprise when she asked her fellow performers about the rude interruption, and they had no idea what she was talking about! With a shiver, the actress realized she had been the only one who had seen the two strangers on the stage. The two *ghosts*, that is.

Today, the building is used by CityArts as an art space, where the paranormal activity continues. In addition to the usual sounds of creaking floorboards and footsteps, people hear knocking sounds from behind the walls, catch orbs of light on film, and feel sudden changes in temperature. Some visitors report a very strong floral scent wafting through the rooms and hallways, almost as if someone wearing perfume has just walked past.

Could it be the scent once favored by Gordon's wife, Magnolia? Some believe so. Magnolia might also be the woman in a white dress who people have seen from time to time, standing on the stairway between the first and second floor, or wandering through the hallways and admiring the building's artwork.

Known to be both friendly and somewhat shy, Magnolia will interact with others in the gallery, studying the art and moving casually through the crowd. Then, she'll make her way to a quiet corner where she can sit by herself for a moment or two before she disappears.

Gordon's ghost has been spotted in the building, too, though less frequently than his wife. When he appears, it is usually as a figure cloaked in shadows, looking out from windows on the second floor. To Gordon, the city beyond the windows must look *very* different, indeed, from the Orlando he remembers.

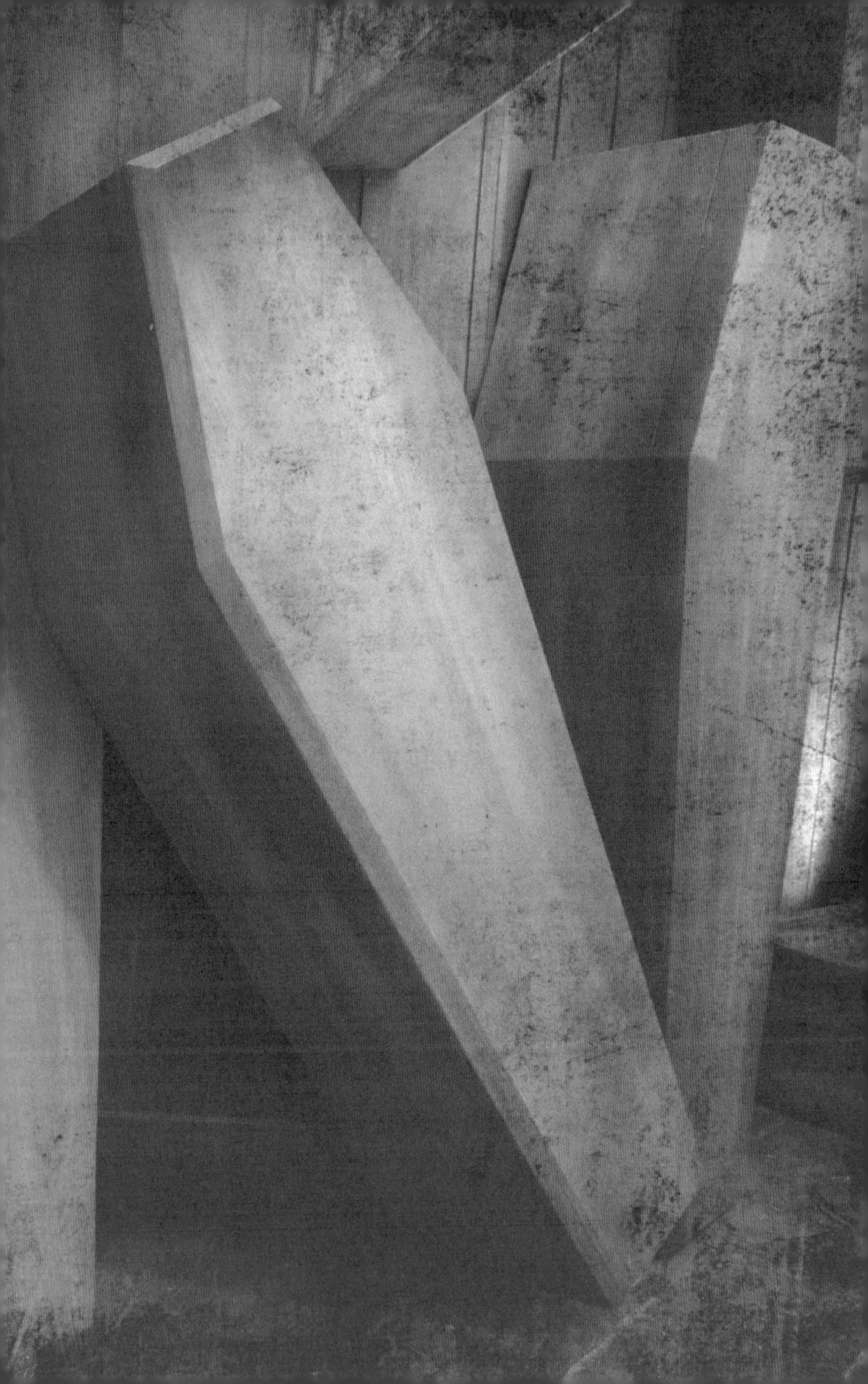

Funerals Were a Business for Two Hands

In the old days, when someone died, their body had to be packed in ice to keep it preserved. That meant funerals had to take place rather quickly because the ice didn't last very long in the Florida heat. And once the ice had melted . . . the bodies didn't last very long, either. (Yikes.) That's how it was in Orlando, until Elijah Hand arrived sometime around

1885, when the small town was beginning to grow into the big city it is today.

Elijah ran the city's main funeral home, where he initially partnered with the city's first undertaker, and then with one of his sons, Carey. Elijah brought something new with him to the funeral business in Orlando: he was the first in town to use embalming, a process that used chemicals to slow down a body's natural decomposition. This meant bodies could be preserved for longer periods of time.

Elijah was also a savvy businessman. He realized that more time before a funeral meant more relatives and friends could attend from out of town. And that meant they would need somewhere to stay. So, he converted the rooms on the second floor of his building into a small hotel.

In those days, people in the funeral business had to have many different skills, including carpentry, since they often had to build coffins for their customers. Elijah expanded his business by making furniture for the living as well as coffins for the dead. (Some say there were so many bodies to prepare that sometimes Elijah would sit them in the chairs he had built and display them in the front window to advertise his work, but I can't say for certain if that is true.)

What I do know is that Elijah's business was very successful and that he left it to his son, Carey, who eventually moved the funeral home across the street from its original location. Like his father, he introduced not one, but two new aspects to the business. His funeral home was the very first in Florida to have its own chapel, and the first south of Washington, D.C., to have its own crematorium.

Both Elijah and Carey are long gone from this life, but perhaps not from the buildings where they worked. In the building where Elijah worked, there have been numerous reports of icy cold spots, the sound of phantom footsteps, and—on the second floor—overwhelming feelings of uneasiness and dread. Some have

complained that the air there feels heavier than it does elsewhere in the building. There have even been sightings of the ghost of a young woman as well as those of small children running through the hallways.

Another spirit residing in the old funeral home might be named Robert—that's what one psychic said after she spent some time there. The name Robert does come up again in a recent story about a woman who worked in the building. She had developed a bond with the business owner's young son, who liked her very much and would come running whenever she called for him. One day, though, the woman called his name and got no response. She knew the boy was somewhere in the building, so she went looking for him, calling out as she went from room to room on the second floor. Eventually, she found him sitting cross-legged in one of the empty offices used for storage. When she asked him what he was doing, he told her with a grin that he was just playing with his friend . . . Mr. Robert. Which leaves us to wonder, was this Mr. Robert imaginary, or was he something else?

In either case, the boy was never again allowed to play alone on the second floor.

Meanwhile, just across the street, the former Carey Hand Funeral Home is now offices for the University of Central Florida, and the spirit activity seems to be a little bit less frequent. Still, people there have heard whispers, footsteps, and other unexplained sounds. And every now and again, late at night on the street between the two funeral homes, some claim to hear the very distinct clomping of a horse's hooves. The sound echoes like one of the same horses that might have transported the dead on their final journey from the funeral homes to the graves.

A Tale of Two Cemeteries

If you are looking for a ghost in Orlando (or anywhere for that matter), one obvious place to look is cemeteries and graveyards. Spirit seekers often explore such places, capturing unexplained orbs of light and mists on their cameras and video recorders, and words, phrases, or other noises on their audio recorders. Sometimes they use spirit boxes, a kind of radio that ghosts can use to communicate with the living. But cemeteries can be as different from one another as the dead buried there. Let's explore two different burial grounds, and you'll see what I mean.

Our first stop is Greenwood Cemetery. Established in the 1880s as one of the area's first public burial places, it spanned twenty-six acres in the heart of the city—which looked very different than it does now. Today, the cemetery is well maintained and frequently visited by those with an interest in history—or ghosts. Many of Orlando's prominent citizens have been laid to rest here, including eight different mayors, a Hall of Fame baseball player, and Elijah and Carey Hand, who ran the funeral business that you read about in another story.

Some of the ghosts at Greenwood include at least a few Confederate soldiers from the Civil War, and the ghost of an older man who appears sometimes out front of the Wilmott family mausoleum. The best-known ghost there, however, is Fred Weeks.

Poor Fred decided to purchase some land on which to build a home for his family before moving to Orlando. But when he arrived, he discovered that the land he'd purchased did not look anything like what he'd been promised. In fact, it was totally worthless swamp land.

Understandably, he was furious about it. At first, the people who sold him the land refused to return his money. So, Fred got creative. He bought a plot in Greenwood Cemetery and had a small mausoleum built on it. (A mausoleum is a large, often stately, above-ground tomb.) On the front door, Fred put a quotation from the Bible about a man who had once been cheated and swindled. Below that, he carved the names of the three men who had scammed him. Those men didn't like having their names listed there.

Having a bad reputation was bad for business. The best thing to do, they decided, was to give Fred his money back and buy his mausoleum so they could remove their names from it.

That might have been the end of the story, but Fred wasn't so sure that those men wouldn't go right back to their dishonest ways. He bought another mausoleum, this one about a hundred feet away from the first one. He left a blank space just big enough for three names, as a reminder to the real estate conmen.

Eventually, Fred passed on and was laid to rest in the second mausoleum. His rest seems to have been short, though, because multiple people have seen him wearing a suit and wandering silently around his monument or through the tombstones nearby as an earthbound soul. Judging by the concerned expression on his face, it seems that even now,

Fred is still very much in the grip of his gripe.

Now, let's take a short drive to another old burial place known as Drawdy-Rouse Cemetery. This one is older than Greenwood by about ten years. It served as a small family plot for the Drawdy family and other pioneer families. This cemetery is not visited as often as Greenwood, and you won't find any famous sports stars, actors and actresses, or political figures here. You won't even find the name of the unfriendly ghost said to haunt this place. Which is why, some say, his spirit is so angry.

According to local legends, one of the pioneers who lived nearby was a man named Benjamin Miles. He lived and died in the area, and was buried in an unmarked grave, which was not so uncommon among pioneers and farmers at the time. As the years passed, people began to take notice of the uncanny feeling they experienced as they walked deeper into the cemetery, toward one of the far corners, where Benjamin's body was believed to be buried. They would feel chills enough to break out in goosebumps, and the hairs on the back of their necks would rise. It felt very much like they were being watched from the shadows.

A local author named Amanda Branham decided to conduct her own investigation during the day. She took pictures of many of the old graves, some of them too weathered and damaged to read. As she made her way into the back half of the cemetery, she called out, "Benjamin Miles, are you here?" The response she got was just one word drawn out like a moan. The word was "*go*." After a terrified moment, she did exactly that. She raced back to the exit and out through the gate, which stood open even though she remembered having closed it. When she got home, she discovered that she had scratches on her face and forehead. Clearly, whatever she had run into in that cemetery did not want to be disturbed. As far as I know, she has not returned there since, and most of the folks who live nearby choose not to go looking for Benjamin Miles anymore, either. Especially not alone or at night.

If you decide to visit any cemeteries or graveyards, here's a bit of advice for you. Legends say that you should never whistle at night in these places because someone or *something* might hear you. If you're lucky, a spirit might give you a good scare by whistling back to let you know they hear you. If you are unlucky, though, a spirit might think that you're calling out to it . . . and leave its resting place to take up residence with you instead.

Annie Russell and the Ghosts of Orlando's Theaters

If you stop to consider it, theaters aren't quite like any other type of building. Even when empty, we can still sense the creativity and wonder that takes place within their walls. Sometimes this is reflected in the décor, which might include the smiling and frowning masks that symbolize comedy and tragedy. The rows of seats around a central stage are designed for us to watch and anticipate what will happen.

Is it possible, though, that things continue to happen even when no one is there to observe them? Late at night, long after the final curtain has been lowered and every living person has left the building—in the dim light of a single bulb near center stage (known as a ghost light)—some people believe that a different set of scenes unfold . . . scenes played by phantoms and spirits.

If you ask around, you might discover that many of Orlando's theaters are said to have ghosts. In Maitland, the Enzian Theater is well known for promoting independent films you might not be able to see elsewhere. The theater is also known for the unexplained things that happen there. It is rumored that on the opening night of new films, and on moonless nights around one o'clock in the morning, something *terrifying* occurs. In the shadowy north corner of the theater, the glowing, transparent head of an unidentified woman suddenly appears, letting loose a bloodcurdling scream as it floats through the room. After appearing and terrifying witnesses, she gradually fades away. Encounters with the screaming head are just one example of the many strange experiences that theater staff have reported.

At 46 North Orange Avenue in downtown Orlando, there's another well-known theater with a haunted history. For more than forty years after it was built in 1873, the building was the first jail and gallows for Orange County. Several prisoners were executed here. According to local legend, after they were hung, the bodies were buried in unmarked graves nearby. That old prison was torn down in 1919. Two years later, on that same spot, Braxton Beacham Sr. built his famous Beacham Theater. Is it possible he discovered a forgotten prison graveyard during the theater's construction?

If so, there is no mention of it, and it did not alter his plans.

The theater was a success, and over the years, it changed to reflect new trends and types of entertainment, from its early days of vaudeville performances, to a movie theater, then a concert hall, and a night club. Even with all those changes, there is still one part of the theater that remains the same: the lightless, sealed tunnels underneath it. These tunnels once connected the theater to a nearby hotel so that performers could come and go without being overwhelmed by crowds. Do the spirits of those hanged prisoners continue to roam the unlit corridors? Were they responsible for the

delays the theater faced when it tried to install a large pipe organ? More importantly, are they still lurking there in the shadows, waiting to make themselves known? Maybe it's best that we keep such questions to ourselves and not go poking around for answers in those deep, dark passageways.

To find the most famously haunted theater in the area, you'll need to head to Winter Park. There, at Rollins College, you can see the Annie Russell Theater, said to be home to the ghost of actress Annie Russell herself. Unlike the ghosts at the Beacham, she doesn't cause any mischief or harm. Most who have encountered her believe she just wants to enjoy the shows

and make sure that the theater named in her honor continues to thrive.

Annie was born in England in the 1860s and moved to Canada when she was still a young girl. By the time she was eight years old, she had already performed in her first play in Montreal. Her family moved to New York, where Annie continued to perform and star in a long list of plays. From there, her success and fame continued to grow until she was one of the best-known actresses of her day.

During this time, she became friends with Mary and Edward Bok. Edward was a successful magazine editor and author who built Bok Tower near Orlando, which you can visit today. Mary suggested that her friend come stay in Winter Park while she recovered from an injury. Annie agreed, and while she was in the area, she happened to watch a play. She realized that Winter Park could use a newer, larger theater, so she and one of her friends proposed the idea to the president of Rollins College. A few years later, Annie was acting on stage at the opening of the new theater she helped create. Sadly, four years later, she died of pneumonia. But as local ghost hunters will tell you, that does not seem to be keeping her from giving an encore performance from beyond the grave.

Why do people think Annie is still there at the theater? There have been sightings of a frail looking female apparition with sad eyes, in a room on the second floor that served as Annie's private changing room. Throughout the building, doors have swung open and shut on their own. Sometimes the folding chair she liked to use when she was watching rehearsals will fold down by itself, as though someone is sitting there. Dogs visiting the theater seem to take notice of that one particular seat. Whenever the seat folds down, though, it is considered a good omen—a sign that Annie's ghost approves of the performance.

Then there's the story of a stagehand who fell from a ladder while working one evening. Luckily, he was there with a friend who found him a short time later and called for an ambulance. The emergency dispatcher said that someone had already called and help was on the way. This was strange, since as far as either the injured man or his friend was aware, they were the only two living people in the theater that night. Was it Annie who had placed the call? Is she still looking after the well-being of those who attend and produce plays in her theater?

Ghost-hunting groups and paranormal investigators have explored the theater. They have recorded strange sounds and voices on their audio equipment, seen orbs of light, and felt changes in temperature and electricity. Such things are to be expected, or course. After all, how could a famous actress possibly resist putting on a show for an audience . . . even if she is no longer among the living?

The Ghosts in the Garden

Not far from the theater Annie Russell haunts, you'll find another pair of ghosts who loved their home so much in life that they've even stuck around after death! These are the spirits of Harry and Mary Jane Leu.

Their story begins more than a hundred and sixty-five years ago with the Mizell family who first settled and built a home in what is now Harry P. Leu Gardens. After the Civil

War, David Mizell became a sheriff and tax collector. His time upholding the law did not last long, though. During a heated argument over cattle—a deadly dispute now known as the Barber-Mizell feud—members of the Barber family ambushed and shot him. David was laid to rest in the small family cemetery that's still on the property today.

After his death, the home was bought by one family after another until it was purchased in 1936 by Harry and Mary Jane Leu. Together, they traveled the world collecting the seeds and sprouts they would eventually use to transform their gardens into a floral wonderland with over two thousand different plants and flowers. Before they passed away, the couple left their property to the city of Orlando so that the public could always visit and enjoy their gardens as much as they did. It seems they are not quite ready to say goodbye to the paradise they created. Inside the family home, many visitors have noticed unusual cold spots, even on the hottest summer days. Phantom footsteps echo, especially on the second-story porch. Some guides who work there have even reported seeing fully formed apparitions of a white-haired, elderly man in a suit, often accompanied by a woman—both appearing and vanishing before their eyes.

There's no reason to be frightened, though. These ghosts do not cause any trouble or mean any harm. It seems like they just want to visit their former home from time to time and make sure their beloved gardens are properly cared for.

While you're at Leu Gardens, you might notice all the Spanish Moss that hangs from the tree branches like long, tangled gray hair. There's a story about how and why that moss came to be in Florida. Long before Florida became a part of the United States, before there were even any white settlers here, the first Europeans to explore the area were the Spaniards known as conquistadors. Famous for their violence and cruelty, the conquistadors craved gold more than anything else on earth, though they never did find very much of it.

According to a legend, one of these Spanish explorers did manage to find a small nugget of gold. He was so obsessed with it that he would often hold it up to the sun to see it shine. One day, as he held it up in his hand, a bird flew by, snatched the gold right out of his fingers, and flew up into a nearby tree. The conquistador was so angry that he climbed up after it, even though he was wearing heavy armor. He chased the bird out onto a tree limb, but it flew up to a higher branch in the tree. Now the conquistador was furious! He kept climbing higher and higher after that bird, but the bird kept that nugget of gold in its beak and stayed just out of reach. Eventually, the conquistador lost his balance and fell. He landed in the crook of a branch where he got stuck and eventually died. But his beard continued to grow! It grew until it covered the entire branch, and then all the branches of the tree. It grew still more, until it hung from the branches of *all* the trees nearby.

Today, that beard—or the silver-gray Spanish Moss that hangs down like a beard from the trees—still grows thick and heavy from every place the greedy conquistadors once touched. The dangling strands wave in the breeze, a beautiful but spooky reminder of an old local legend. At least, that's what some folks around here say, anyhow.

Maitland Art Center Gardens

Two More Ghostly Caretakers

It probably seems like something of a theme by now, how ghosts like to look in on the places they enjoyed when they were alive. We've seen this pattern with Gordon and Magnolia Rogers, with Harry and Mary Jane Leu, with Gertrude Sweet, and with Annie Russell. We're about to add a few more names to that list, and we'll start by traveling just north of Orlando to Maitland.

There are plenty of fun things to do in Maitland. You can see a movie at the Enzian Theater or spend the day learning about various birds at the Audubon Center for Birds of Prey. One of my favorite ways to spend the day in Maitland is to see all the wondrous new artwork and galleries at the Art and History Center of Maitland. The museums and art galleries there are all connected, built in a style inspired by ancient Mayan temples. If you're lucky, you might run into its founder, André Smith. He has been known to show up every once in a while—a pretty neat trick considering he died there in 1959!

Visitors, staff, and local artists have spotted him wandering through the studios and outside between the buildings. Maybe André also visits to give the artists some inspiration. One artist named James Cook, who made beautiful pottery, was sure that he heard André's voice one afternoon. The ghostly conversation sounded as if André was discussing James's artwork with someone else, pointing out ways it could be improved. Curious rather than frightened, James decided to follow the ghostly advice. He tried something different, taking a new approach to his pottery style, and can you guess what happened? His new creations became quite successful!

Another artist said that he once heard the sound of glass breaking behind him. He spun around just in time to see the transparent form of André standing there for a moment before fading away. One of the former heads of the Art Center once showed up to work early and noticed a man standing out back. When she went out to investigate, nobody was there—the figure had completely vanished. She, like many people who've had similar experiences, believes that man was André, returning to check on how his little art colony has blossomed into the very special and creative place it is today.

While visiting the Art Center, you should take a short walk to the Waterhouse Residence—the oldest home in Maitland and what some people have called the most haunted home in central Florida. Now converted into a museum, the house offers visitors a glimpse into what daily family life was like more than a hundred years ago.

William Waterhouse built the house in 1884, where he lived with his wife, Sarah, and their two children, Charles and Stella. Stella grew up and grew old in that house, remaining there until she was in her nineties. Lots of people have seen a woman dressed in old-fashioned clothing standing behind a window on the second floor, looking out over Lake Lilly. Most agree that it's the ghost of Stella, still lingering in the only home she ever knew. According to local guides and volunteers, Stella still has very strong opinions about how her bedroom should look. She has a habit of moving furniture around—usually when no one is watching—but at least one person claims to have seen the bed moving on its own across the floor.

As you may have already realized, ghosts and spirits are often quite particular about how things should be, especially in the places they've lived and loved. That brings us to our next ghost and his feline friend. You will find the captain and his cat in Longwood at a rather unusual-looking building that is sometimes called the Inside-Outside House. This unique building earned its nickname because it looks like the house was put together the wrong way, with its skeleton on the outside and stucco walls inside. But it's not a mistake—that was its intended design when it was first built in Massachusetts before being taken apart, shipped to Florida, and reassembled where captain W. Pierce, his wife, and his cat, Brutus, lived together until they passed away.

Another family lived in the home for a short time, and after that, the home sat empty, collecting dust and stories. People whispered about voices coming from empty rooms and hallways, and glimpsed a black cat in one of the upstairs windows that vanished when they approached. Some said they felt, but could not see, a small animal like a cat brushing up against their legs. They supposed it was the ghost of Brutus, still patrolling his favorite haunts.

After many years,

a woman named Pamela bought the home with her husband. On the first floor, they have a store called the Cottage Gift Shop. Though Pamela had heard some rumors of hauntings before purchasing the home, she didn't believe them until her own unexplainable experiences began.

One evening, she carefully placed a crystal bowl on the mantle before locking up the shop for the night. When she returned the next morning, she found the bowl on the floor underneath a table but not broken. *That's strange*, she thought. It was almost as if someone had placed it there on purpose.

Not long after, she found a miniature replica of the Inside-Outside House at the foot of the stairway. She didn't recall having left the little collectible there—it was as if someone had been sitting on the steps, examining it.

Another afternoon, while Pamela was on the second floor, she felt a sudden intense chill sweep through the room, even though the air conditioning was turned off. In that moment, she felt very strongly that someone was there with her and wanted her to leave. She loudly announced that she was leaving the room, and that is exactly what she did.

As time went by, the evidence of haunting only grew: the ghostly silhouette of a man appeared standing by a table near the door; a gruff voice spoke directly behind Pamela in an otherwise empty room; and one night while working alone, Pamela heard a door open and close loudly. Thinking her husband had arrived, she called their home phone. When he answered, she realized she truly was alone in the building. (Or was she?)

When she looks back on these experiences, Pamela is convinced that each time, it was the work of Captain Pierce alongside his cat Brutus. It seems the pair never truly left their beloved home, even if they mostly (thankfully) keep to themselves. Every once in a while, they will do something to let Pamela know that they are still there. But for the most part, Pamela, the Captain, and his cat have all made their peace with each other and are comfortable sharing the space.

206

A Haunted Hotel

If you're like me, I bet you enjoy going on vacation. It's great fun and exciting to go someplace new and see and do things you've never done before. After a long day, isn't it wonderful to come back to a nice hotel room and sink into a bed so soft that it feels like you're lying on a cloud? But what if you started to sense that you weren't alone in that room? What if you got the feeling that someone or something was watching you there? What if the lights began to flicker, and the faucet in the bathroom turned itself on and off? What if you heard footsteps coming close to that bed you were lying on? Worst of all, what if you felt someone you could not see lie down right beside you, and even noticed the impression of their body in those soft sheets? What would you do if that happened?

If that sounds like a made-up story, I assure you, it is very real to all the people who had that experience in room number 206 at a hotel in Orlando. Since the hotel's management and staff would like to keep the story quiet, out of respect for them, I'm not going to tell you which hotel it is. You'll simply have to make sure your next Orlando hotel room isn't already occupied by someone who checked out years ago . . . but never actually left.

Some hotels are more haunted than others. There was one in downtown Orlando that was especially welcoming to guests from the great beyond. That hotel was the Angebilt, which opened in 1923 with 250 rooms. Even though it was a first-class hotel when it was built, the Angebilt suffered many difficulties over the years, including damage from fires and hurricanes. Eventually, the hotel closed and was converted into an office building. However, it seems that some of the former guests never received their final bill because strange things continue to happen throughout the building to this day.

Much of the ghostly activity seems to involve the bathrooms. Witnesses report bathroom stalls suddenly locking, shaking, and rattling with great force while someone is inside—as if someone is desperately trying to enter. One terrified person unable to unlock the rattling door chose to crawl out underneath the stall door to escape.

Another incident involves a woman who was working alone late one night. After returning from the bathroom to her office, she shut the door behind her, only to watch it slowly and eerily creak back open a moment later. Thinking it had to be a problem with the latch, she shut the door again, locked it, and tried the handle to make sure it was secure. Satisfied, she returned again to her desk, but the door mysteriously unlocked itself and began swinging open and closed repeatedly. Because the air conditioning was turned off, there was no draft in the building, so the woman could not understand or explain how or why the door was behaving the way it did. In any case, she did not wait around to find out! She packed up her belongings, turned off her computer, and left as fast as she could. As far as I know, local sources say she has never worked alone at night in the Angebilt building again. And really . . . do you blame her?

Spirits of the Deep

Sometimes ghosts are attached to an object rather than a place. If you think about it, just about *anything* could have a ghost connected to it—a toy, a baseball card, a comb, a dress . . . even this very book! But usually, the connection is strongest with the things someone might have been carrying when they died, especially if they met their end tragically.

One example of this involves a very famous boat that people said could never be sunk. But they were wrong—it *did* sink, after colliding with an iceberg on April 14, 1912. Do you know what doomed ship I'm referring to? If you said, "the *Titanic*," then you would be correct. Well, did you know there is a place in Orlando where you can see many of the real objects that were on that ship when it sank? On International

Drive, you will find *Titanic: The Artifact Exhibition*. Along with the objects on display, you might also run into spirits still not ready to be parted from those objects.

Since the museum first opened, there have been flickering lights and unexpected changes in temperature that no one has been able to fix. Orbs of light often appear on cameras and videos, and every now and then, people have complained about the overpowering briny, saltwater scent of the ocean.

Visitors and staff claim to have seen apparitions and ghosts wandering from room to room between exhibits. One is of a man with a big, bushy beard who looks very much like a newspaper editor who perished on the ship when it sank. Could his spirit still be trying to send one final headline from beyond the grave? Another frequent apparition is the spirit of a young girl who appears to be about seven years old. If you see her, she might give your clothing a tug, or move things from one room to another, or bang metal objects together loudly. Some believe this is the ghost of Catherine Johnson, who was just seven years old when she and her family traveled in third class aboard the Titanic. She can be quite mischievous. To keep her occupied, the staff at the Titanic exhibit have given young Catherine

her own Raggedy Ann doll to play with, which they leave out for her in places where she won't disturb any living visitors.

Are there other ghosts at the museum? Many of the people who work there believe there are. Sometimes they offer ghost tours, so you can decide for yourself. That's really the best way to dive deeper into the matter. For now, let's you and I just keep to the surface, where it's nice and safe.

CHAPTER 11

Ghosts of the Theme Parks

If you're visiting the Orlando area, one of the most popular activities is enjoying a theme park—especially Walt Disney World. With its cast of beloved characters like Mickey and Minnie Mouse, thrilling rides like Space Mountain and the Haunted Mansion, unforgettable performances, sweet treats, and other special events, the park is known around the globe and draws people from all walks of life. Even, some might say, the *afterlife*.

Long after the sun has set behind Cinderella's castle, the nightly fireworks have faded from view, the shops and rides have closed, and the Magic Kingdom has emptied of living guests, the park comes alive for a different, far spookier kind of guest.

Over the decades, many tales of strange happenings and hauntings—especially late at night—have become a fascinating part of Disney lore. Inside the Haunted Mansion, where phantom footsteps echo and strange faces appear in mirrors, three specific spirits are known to make regular appearances. First is the dapperly dressed man known as "the Tuxedo Ghost." He likes to sneak up behind unsuspecting cast members, place one of his ice-cold hands on their shoulders, and give them a scare they won't soon forget. The second is the ghost of a little boy who seems happy to just ride the attractions and keep to himself, though visitors have captured photographs of him peeking over the side of a "Doom Buggy." The third apparition, a man with a cane, is particularly mysterious. When cast members approach him, he simply vanishes into thin air. Some people think he might have been a World War II pilot who died when his plane crashed nearby.

There have been other uncanny occurrences in the park. In the caves on Tom Sawyer Island, many visitors and cast members have described overwhelming sensations of dread while witnessing shadows that appear to move on their own, unattached to any living thing. A mischievous doll named Isabella is rumored to haunt Liberty Square, appearing mysteriously behind different store windows. Inside the *It's a Small World* attraction, various figures are said to come to life and continue moving, even after the power has been turned off.

But among Disney World's countless spooks and specters, the most well-known ghost by far is George, a spirit who likes to cause trouble at the *Pirates of the Caribbean* ride, where he reportedly met his *own* unfortunate end. You won't find much documentation about George. You won't even learn his last name. There are different and conflicting stories about him, but they all begin around 1973, when Walt Disney World and the *Pirates of the Caribbean* ride were under construction. The story goes that one of the construction workers was a man named George. He was putting together a tower for the "burning city" portion of the ride when disaster struck. Some claim George fell from the top of a tall ladder, while others say a heavy metal beam broke loose and landed on his head. In either case, the result was that George died instantly.

Though workers carried his lifeless body from the site of the accident, George's spirit has remained behind. Shortly after the ride first opened, cast members noticed his initials carved into the same tower George had been working on. They painted over the letters, but a short time later—to everyone's shock—the initials reappeared in the exact same place. For a second time, workers painted over the initials, and once again, the letters soon reappeared. No matter how often the initials were painted over, they *always* returned. That is why it's now called "George's tower."

But this is only the start of his ghostly activity. When it comes to many of the malfunctions and breakdowns on the ride, George is usually the prime suspect—especially when the park's engineers can't find anything wrong with the machinery or electronics. The good news is, George usually gives some warning signs before he's planning to make mischief. If a light in his tower goes on, or if the door suddenly opens behind the animatronic dog with the prison keys in its mouth, visitors can expect long lines and delays (and cast members can expect lots of complaints).

Visitors have also experienced intense cold spots and disembodied whispers coming from empty seats on the ride—sometimes even from right beside them! Now and then, security cameras will capture strange, blurry images that no one can explain.

So, what do the cast members do to make sure George is content not to disturb Disney guests? They say good morning to him at the beginning of each day, and goodnight before locking the doors. As long as this tradition is upheld, the ride operates smoothly, and George is content to keep to himself rather than cause too much mischief. Mostly.

Creepy Tales from Around Orlando

You're probably familiar with the famous Washington Irving story about a real place called Sleepy Hollow, located in New York. In that story, a ghost known as the Headless Horseman terrorizes a man named Ichabod Crane. If I told you that there is a similar story right here in Florida, would you believe me?

There are many different versions of this old local legend from the Kissimmee area. In one, a young man was caught stealing cattle. The cattle owners were so enraged that they decided to get justice for themselves. They hanged him from the branches of a huge oak tree, now known as Dead Man's Tree. The body hung there so long that eventually it was nothing more than a skeleton. When it fell apart, the skull rolled away.

In another version of the story, the man wasn't trying to steal cattle but rather escape from Spanish soldiers. It's not clear if he was a spy or had committed some other crime, but those soldiers were eager to catch him. They cornered him and tied him to Dead Man's Tree and lopped his head off.

Well, according to local lore, the headless man kept on searching for his head, even after his death! Years ago, some people claimed to have seen a ghostly headless horseman circling the old oak tree on moonlit nights. He never seemed to notice anyone around him and just kept riding in circles around the tree, searching for the topmost part of himself. No one has seen him in twenty-five years, though. So maybe, at long last, he succeeded in locating his severed head and can finally rest in peace, rather than pieces.

Have you ever heard the legend of the Oviedo Ghost Lights? Locals might also describe them as the Chuluota Lights. For more than seventy years, people have told stories about strange balls of light they encounter near the bridge over the Econlockhatchee River. Usually appearing during summer months, between midnight and one o'clock, unexplained glowing orbs have been observed rising from the water and hanging suspended in the air. They don't always stay still, though—some people claim to have been chased away from the water when those lights came swarming at them like angry fireflies!

Though this phenomenon is not new, no one really knows what they are or what they want. Could they be the spirits of people who lost their lives somewhere nearby, whether the restless spirits of drowning victims or the ghosts of lovelorn men and women who jumped from the bridge?

Maybe there's a more rational explanation. Some folks think the orbs are just swamp gas, bubbling up from the water. Still, others believe it might be the headlights of distant cars creating a ghostly illusion on the road. If you ask anyone who has been chased by the spectral lights, though, they will tell you that whatever the orbs really are, they do *not* act like any gas bubble or trick of light. On the contrary, it seemed to those people that the lights were intelligent and wanted them *gone*. If you see those strange, swirling orbs, best not disturb them. And if they start coming your way, run!

Speaking of places you might want to avoid, everyone knows highways can be very dangerous, but do you believe that a highway can be haunted? That's what some say about

one part of Interstate 4, or I-4, known as the Dead Zone. Long before there was ever a highway there, a man named Henry Sanford tried to build a small community called St. Joseph's Colony. Don't bother trying to find that place on a map. It's long gone now. Only four families ever moved there, and they did not stay long. One of those families became sick with yellow fever and four of them died. Because the local priest was far away at the time, the members of that unfortunate family were buried without ceremony in a small plot.

Years later, when a farmer bought the land, he thought it was best to just leave those graves alone. In time, however, people began calling it "the field of the dead." Then, the State of Florida bought the land to build a highway. Instead of moving those graves, they built the road right on top of them. As you can imagine, the spirits of that family were not very happy about it. All sorts of unusual things started happening, including a major hurricane tearing across the state and back! The eye of that storm passed right over the highway, which was under construction at the time.

Since the road was completed, many drivers have had trouble with their phones, radios, and other electronics whenever they pass over that spot where the graves are believed to be. A few people have even claimed to see a family of four walking along the side of the highway. But they always seem to vanish after just a moment.

The small patch of I-4 where the graves were located has become one of the deadliest parts of that highway. So, when you are leaving Orlando, be careful. There might still be ghosts on the road ahead.

A Ghostly Goodbye

It looks like our spooky journey together has come to an end—for now. It's been quite a ride, hasn't it? We've found ghosts in theaters, hotel beds, and on amusement park rides. We've visited graveyards and museums and peered through the cobwebs into many of Orlando's historic old buildings. I bet you've had your fill of ghosts for a while. But if you find yourself wanting *more* ghostly tales about other haunted places, just keep on traveling down the road from Orlando. It might take you to Tampa, Miami, St. Augustine, Tallahassee, or Key West. All those places have their own ghosts, and those ghosts have their own stories to tell. Come to think of it, I don't think I've ever visited a city that didn't have at least one spooky story to share. Keep that in mind, and no matter where you are and where you go, if you continue to search for ghosts and ghouls

and other things that go bump in the night, you can be certain that either you will find them, or they will find you.

JOSHUA GINSBERG is a writer, entrepreneur, and curiosity seeker, who in 2016, decided with his wife to trade in the frigid winters of the Midwest for the year-round sunshine of Tampa Bay. He has had numerous published works of poetry, fiction, and non-fiction, and has been a business proposal writer and professional resume writer for over ten years. He currently lives in Tampa's Town and Country neighborhood with his wife, Jen, and their Shih Tzu, Tinker Bell.

Check out some of the other *Spooky America* titles available now!

Spooky America was adapted from the creeptastic *Haunted America* series for adults. *Haunted America* explores historical haunts in cities and regions across America. Here's more from the original *Haunted Orlando* author, Joshua Ginsberg: